# Outdated Advertising

# Outdated Advertising

Sexist, Racist, Creepy, and Just Plain Tasteless Ads from a Pre-PC Era

Compiled and edited by
**Michael Lewis** and **Stephen Spignesi**

Foreword by Ben B. Judd Jr.

Skyhorse Publishing

Skyhorse Publishing books may be purchased in bulk at special discounts for sales promotion, corporate gifts, fund-raising, or educational purposes. Special editions can also be created to specifications. For details, contact the Special Sales Department, Skyhorse Publishing, 307 West 36th Street, 11th Floor, New York, NY 10018 or info@skyhorsepublishing.com.

Skyhorse® and Skyhorse Publishing® are registered trademarks of Skyhorse Publishing, Inc.®, a Delaware corporation.

Visit our website at www.skyhorsepublishing.com.

10 9 8 7 6 5 4 3

Library of Congress Cataloging-in-Publication Data is available on file.

Cover design by Rain Saukas
Cover photos from editors' collection

Print ISBN: 978-1-5107-2380-1
Ebook ISBN: 978-1-5107-2382-5

Printed in China

# Dedications

## Michael

I dedicate this book to my coauthor, Steve. It's been a real pleasure working with you for more than two decades, as editor, collaborator, consultant, therapist, sounding board, etc. Our relationship is what publishing is all about and I look forward to our creative endeavors in the future.

## Stephen

This book is dedicated to the women who persisted,
even after getting in trouble for buying the wrong coffee.

# Contents

# Foreword
## by Ben B. Judd Jr., PhD

From the earliest times, merchants have used some form of promotion to sell their wares.

Early promotions ranged from the farmer in the village square positioning his best fruit at the front of his booth to shopkeepers displaying painted images outside, such as wooden loaves of bread at the baker or shoes at the cobbler. But the beginning of mass advertising as we know it resulted from the invention of the printing press around the year 1500. Printed ads could then reach hundreds or millions of potential customers. Some of these five hundred years of advertising have been preserved for our enjoyment and amazement. This book captures some of that history—creativity and misfires all.

The selected ads also represent the evolution of our culture and technology. One of the earliest advertisements in the set, introducing a strange liquid—coffee from Turkey—is worth a giggle. Two ads from the early history of the American colonies have dramatically different effects on modern sensibilities: one from 1609 offering fruit trees for farmers (practical and benign) and one from the 1800s listing slave auctions for the plantation (repulsive). In the early twentieth century, we find a magic lotion that will "wash away fat" in a few weeks (useless) and cocaine drops to relieve a toothache (dangerous). Varied images of women are presented in the ads: needing a deodorizing soap to catch a man, using a corset for beauty, pleasing your husband with great coffee, nude poses around a stereo speaker, Rosie the Riveter, the clever secretary. As for technology, we see the first TVs, the beginning of long-distance telephone systems, the first computers, and the first "advanced" word processor—all hilariously primitive by today's standards.

Beyond the history that is represented in the selected ads, we find curious and often offensive copy.

- Will a woman considering a weight-reducing diet drink be enticed by a selection of wigs to change her personality?
- Is 7Up soda a good baby food?
- Do babies prefer that mothers smoke Marlboro cigarettes?
- Should a black "Rastus," who can't spell, be a spokesman for Cream of Wheat?
- Should toddlers be handling loaded guns to demonstrate safety locks?
- Does a man need a pamphlet on how to spank his wife?
- How about a fake hand grenade to scare your friends?

# Outdated Advertising

These and worse are all here.

How to explain some of the misfiring messages in these ads? Some messages reflect the contemporary science of their day. Before the 1930s almost any potion was permitted as a patent medicine; magic tonics or devices were widely sold by enterprising hucksters. Cigarettes were claimed to be healthy. Chewing gum was a digestive aid. No claims had to be substantiated by testing and there were few money-back guarantees. In the electronics sphere, technology evolved quickly. The first TV remote controls were quasi-mechanical devices that switched the power cord. The spokesperson for an early pocket computer was a science fiction writer.

Another source of offensive or jarring messaging might be described as a targeting problem. Today an ad copywriter defines his or her target audience, say middle-aged males, and then selects magazines primarily read by that audience. A message appealing to that specific audience might be appalling to others. Consider the ad with a baby playing with a loaded revolver: dad focuses on the safety features while mom is horrified. Or, think about the ad for men's ties with a wife bringing breakfast to her husband in bed, with a tagline advising him to "show her it's a man's world." That might have worked in a men's magazine but not in a woman's fashion mag. Early advertisers were not always able to selectively target.

An additional tricky subject is fantasy, which is a culturally bound appeal. One ad for men's slacks depicts a woman's body as a rug and the man's foot posed on top of her head. It claims that one look at their Dacron slacks will "floor" the girl so you can "walk all over her." Another fantasy appeal, typical of cigarette ads, is that a man offering a woman the right smoke will get her right to bed. Not all women would respond positively to this idea. For women, a similar fantasy might be that adding or losing a few pounds to your bust will get the man.

Finally, modern copywriters have learned that images of smiling customers are much more important than wordy text. Fewer words provide less opportunity for confusion or offense. The old ads may have dozens of words depicting multiple performance claims for a product; the more one reads, the greater the disbelief. Modern ads usually focus on a picture with a mini-drama, such as parents showing pride over their handsome son. That scene avoids any message other than "your son looks great in Dockers."

Enjoy the ads.

**Ben B. Judd Jr.**, PhD, is the former chair of the University of New Haven Department of Marketing and International Business, and the associate dean of the University of New Haven School of Business. During his career, Dr. Judd taught many courses on marketing research, e-commerce, retailing, and consumer behavior, including "Principles of Marketing," "Consumer Marketing," and "Advertising and Promotion."

He has also written extensively on advertising, global business, and new developments in trade and marketing. Some of his published essays include "Do Nudes in Ads Enhance Brand Recall?," which appeared in the *Journal of Advertising Research*; "Differences in Attitudes Toward Nudity in Advertising," which appeared in *Psychology* magazine; and "On the Reduced Effectiveness of Some Sexually Suggestive Ads," which appeared in the *Journal of the Academy of Marketing Science*.

He served as a consultant to a wide array of organizations, industrials, and private enterprises, including media outlets, retail establishments, and cities.

Dr. Judd is now retired and devotes time to research and writing. He lives in Bethany, Connecticut.

# Introduction

Times have certainly changed since the days when the ads in this book were published.

We, your authors, are savvy guys. We're wild and crazy writers and editors; we like to think we've been around and that we've seen it all. (Or at least some of it all.)

Well, no.

Some of the ads in this book are the Merriam-Webster definition of *egregious*: "conspicuously bad; flagrant."

We can also add *surprising* as an apropos adjective for some of what you'll see in these pages, specifically the ones seen through 20/20 hindsight: OJ Simpson running from . . . something; Michael Jackson shilling a record player for children; pre-Caitlyn Bruce Jenner working out.

People who have seen some of these ads, peeking over our shoulders while we were working on this book, usually had two specific responses to seeing them:

1. Wow.
2. Are you ****** kidding me?

But when the ads originally ran, in a different day, with a different public mind-set, maybe they weren't quite as startling, shocking, or laughable. And that's the point of this book—it's a snapshot of a different age.

We do not comment on these images. We didn't need to: the ads speak for themselves.

These ads are eye-openers. And if you're like us, you will never look at Santa, a bottle of 7Up, or a pear the same way again.

These ads are not politically correct. You are guaranteed to find some of them offensive. But don't write to the companies that produced these ads.

They are a product of their time, and at that time most people had no problem with them. And the few who did had little recourse other than sending a letter that was likely ignored. (In today's social media world, people can quickly and effectively let advertisers know when they've crossed the line.)

Don't do that. Instead, just shake your head, reflect on how we have indubitably changed, and turn the page.

—Michael Lewis
Stephen Spignesi

**1609**

**1652**

# Celebrity Endorsements

## Bruce Jenner, 1979

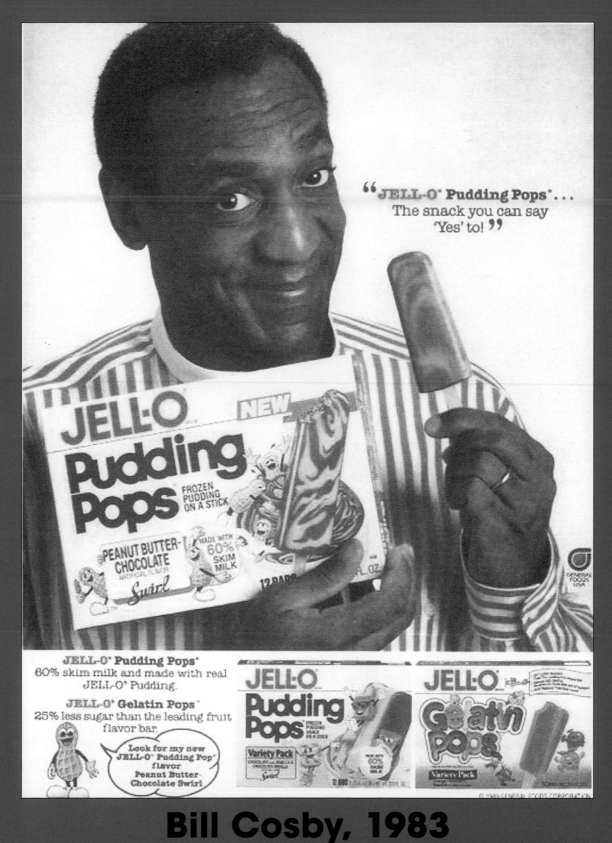

**Bill Cosby, 1983**

OJ Simpson, 1975

"On business trips these days, you've got to make every minute, every dollar count!

That's why you need Hertz more than ever."

*OJ Simpson*

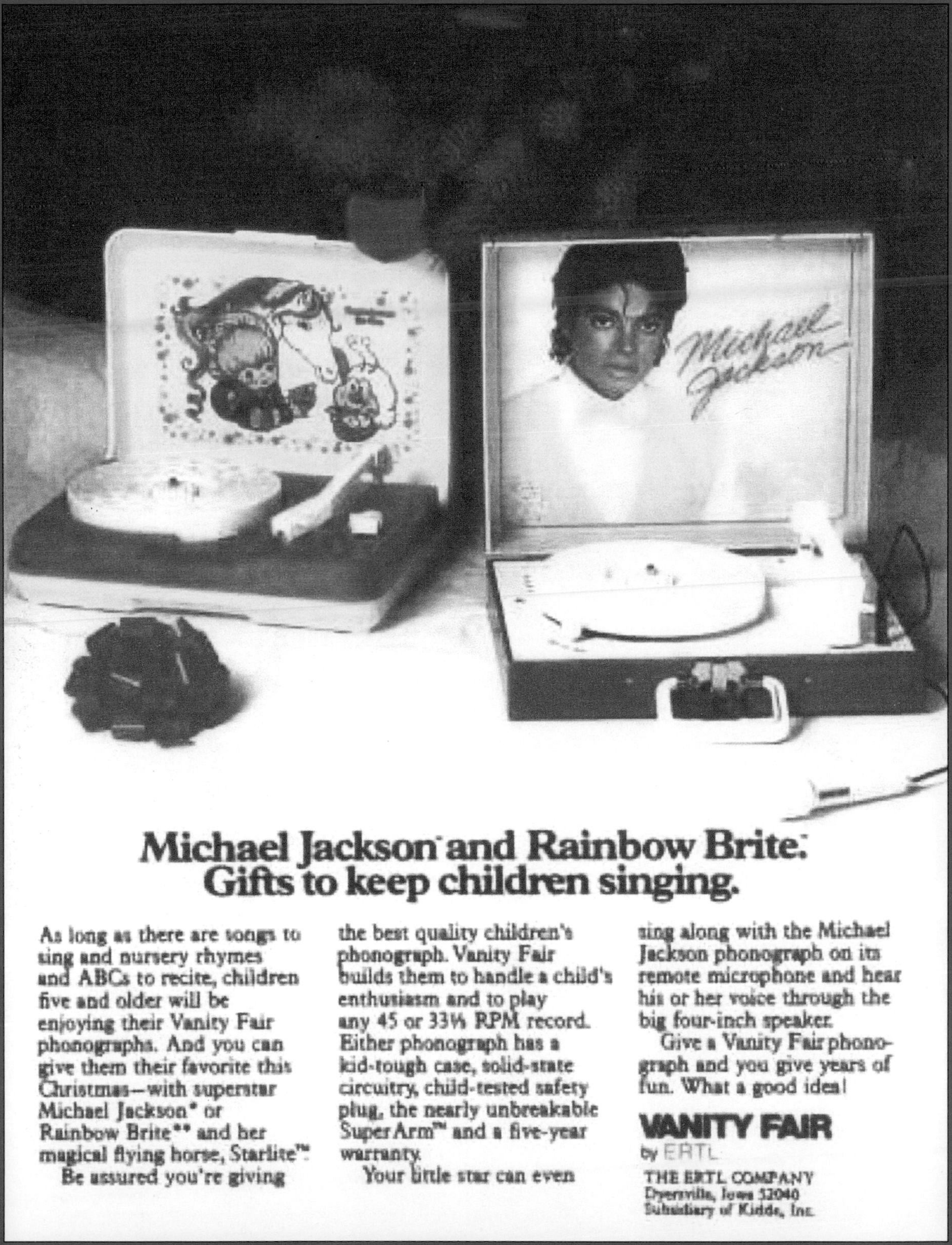


**Michael Jackson, 1984**

**Alice Cooper, 1973**

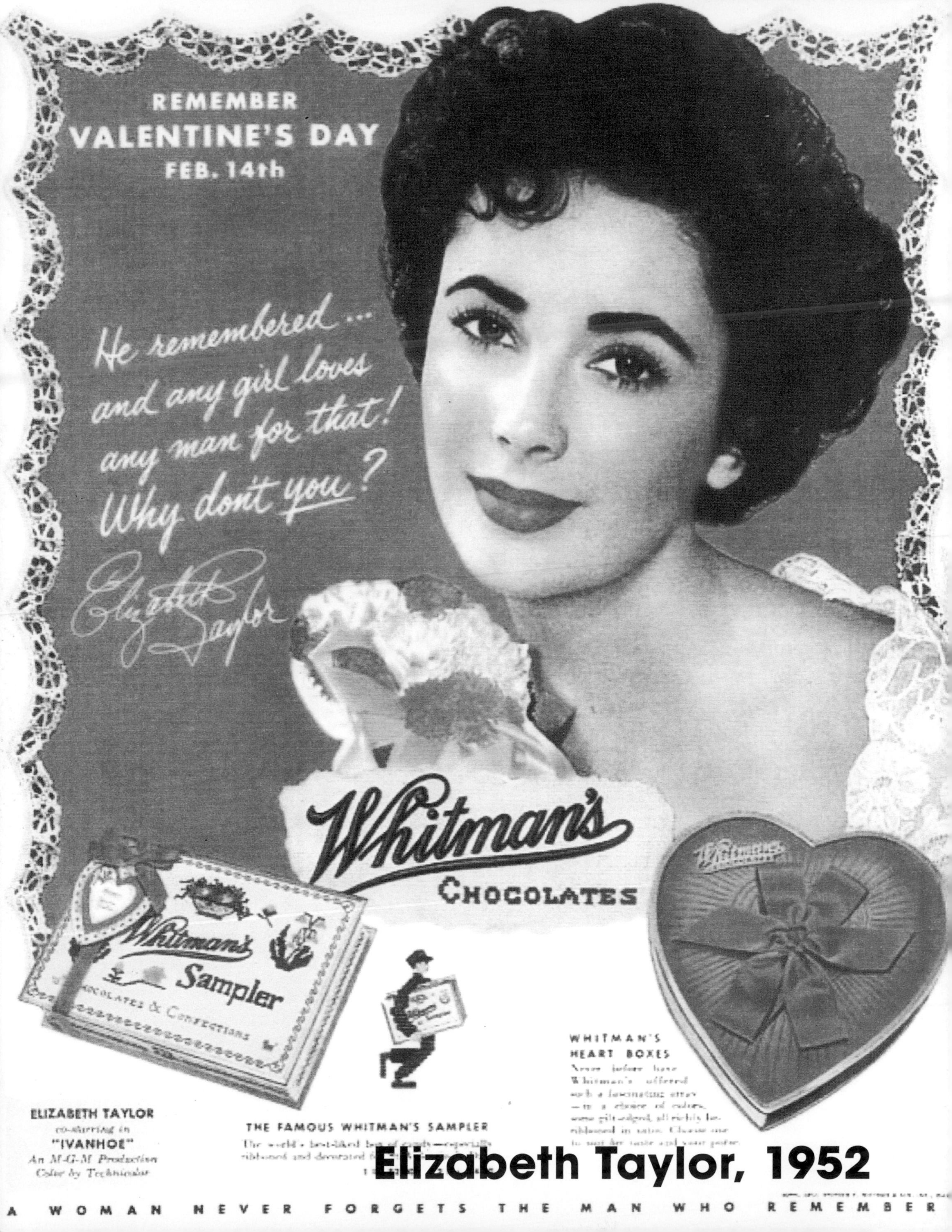


Elizabeth Taylor, 1952

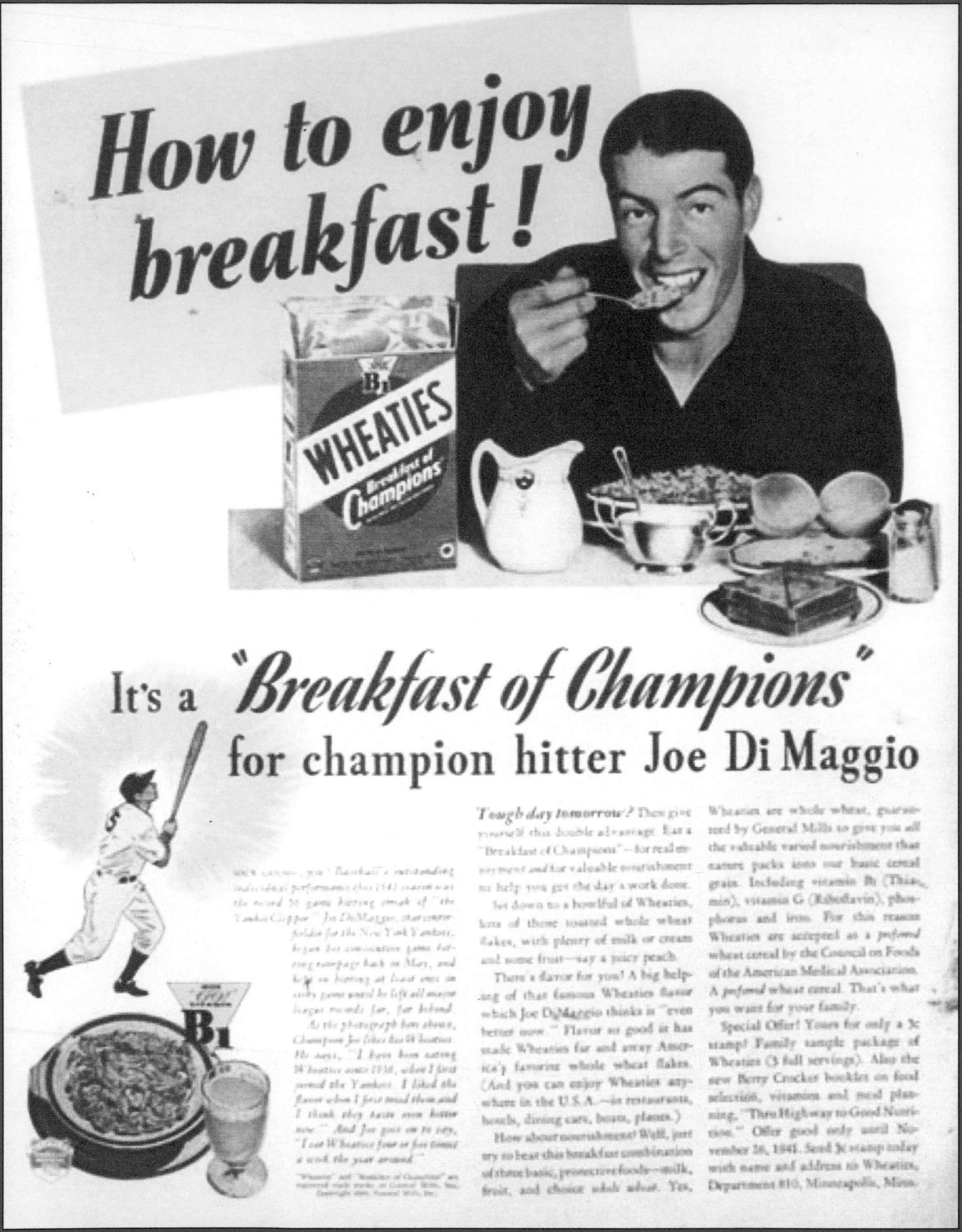


Joe DiMaggio, 1941

**Frank Zappa, 1967**

Shirley Temple, 1945

## Andy Warhol, 1974

TONY THE TIGER SAYS:

## "You bet your life they're Gr-r-reat!"

No wonder Groucho's speechless. What if a tiger stole your microphone and your favorite line. But that's Tony for you. And he's all for you when he tells you to try these big, crackly flakes of corn. Because they're the ones with the secret Kellogg's sugar coating all over. Gr-r-reat? You bet your life.

*Kellogg's* SUGAR FROSTED FLAKES

# Groucho Marx, 1955

Bob Hope, 1961

Kodak EKTRA camera

1

# Give a Can-Do camera for less than $18.

Take it easy with the Kodak Ektra 1 camera.
Easy to use, and at this price, even easier to give.
Make someone happy this Christmas with
an Ektra camera for sharp, clear pictures.

Kodak

OFFICIAL PHOTO CONSULTANT TO
THE 1980 OLYMPIC WINTER GAMES.

Price is subject to change without notice. ©Eastman Kodak Company, 1979

Found in Mom's Basement

Kodak gifts say
"open me first"
...to save Christmas
in pictures.

# Michael Landon, 1979

# I'm not entering any beauty contests. So why do I use a skin moisturizer?

—Joe Namath

Because shaving, wind, weather and old man sunshine can make a man's skin feel dry, chapped and uncomfortable.

That's why a man needs new Brut 33 Skin Moisturizer. It's a greaseless lotion containing twelve moisturizing ingredients that are quickly absorbed by the skin.

Brut 33 Skin Moisturizer can do for a man's skin what a workout can do for his body. Condition it. Tone it. Make it feel good all over.

And like all physical fitness programs, skin care works best when you stick with it. Just rub a little Brut 33 Skin Moisturizer into your face, hands and body every

time you shower or shave. Even one application can help make your rough, dry skin feel smooth and comfortable again. (If it makes your skin look better too, don't complain.)

Brut 33 Skin Moisturizer for men, from Fabergé. Because being rough and tough doesn't mean your skin has to feel that way.

## Brut 33 Skin Moisturizer
Physical fitness for a man's skin.

© 1977 FABERGE, INC.

## Joe Namath, 1977

Tom Selleck, 1981

CHAZ

CHAZ
COLOGNE FOR MEN

The fragrance that's almost as interesting as the men who wear it

CHAZ for men by Revlon. Cologne, After Shave, Soap and Talc.

# Cigarettes

**1936**

**1947**

**1948**

I'M SENDING CHESTERFIELDS to all my friends.
That's the merriest Christmas any smoker can have —
Chesterfield mildness plus no unpleasant after-taste

*Ronald Reagan*

see RONALD REAGAN
starring in "HONG KONG" a Pine-
Thomas Paramount Production
Color by Technicolor

CHESTERFIELD *Buy the beautiful "Christmas-card" carton*

**1949**

Smoke for Pleasure
today —
No Cigarette Hangover
tomorrow!
Remember:
Call for PHILIP MORRIS
You'll be glad tomorrow . . . you smoked PHILIP MORRIS today!

**1952**

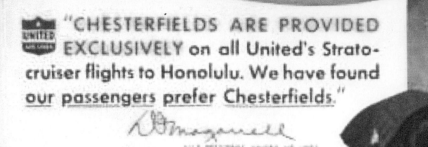

1954

1951

# Sexist Ads

1952

# 4 channel sound means 4 speakers in one room

Empire Grenadier speakers blend with any decor. Made to order for modern four channel living. You will be amazed at the sound clarity and wide angle dispersion. From $109.95 at better hi fi dealers. Write for your "Empire Guide to Sound Design."

World Famous Speaker Systems
Mfd. U.S.A.

Dept. Y, 1055 Stewart Avenue
Garden City, New York 11530

## 1972

**Should a gentleman offer a Tiparillo to a violinist?**

After a tough evening with the Beethoven crowd, she loves to relax and listen to her folk-rock records. Preferably, on *your* stereo. She's open-minded. So maybe tonight you offer her a Tiparillo®. She might like it—the slim cigar with a white tip. Elegant. And, you dog, you've got both kinds on hand. Tiparillo Regular and new Tiparillo M with menthol—her choice of mild smoke or cold smoke. Well? Should you offer? After all, if she likes the offer, she might start to play. No strings attached.

**1967**

**1951**

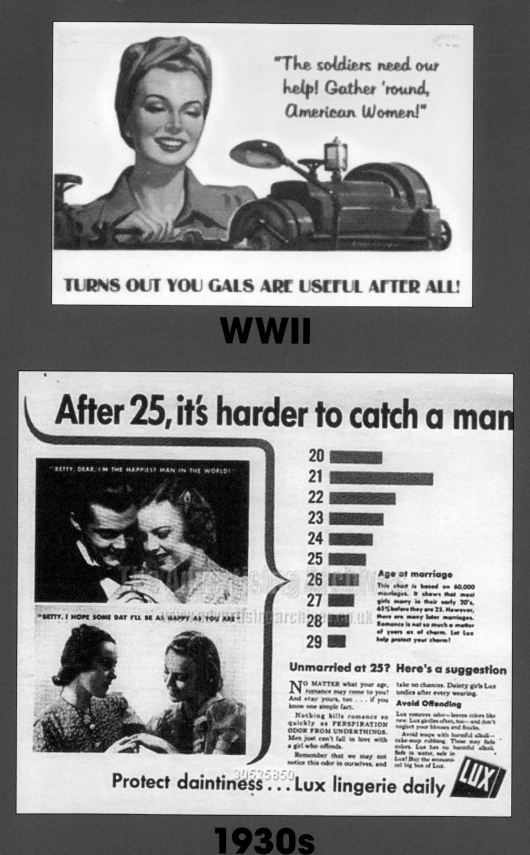

**WWII**

**1930s**

# Just 1 minute, Young Lady!

We overheard that plaint . . . "If my hair looks such a mess *one more* night, I'll kill myself!" So give us *one* minute! Because Charles Antell guarantees that in just one minute Formula 9 will give you healthier-looking, more beautiful hair. And this guarantee is unconditional!

Frankly, you're going to use something on your hair. Everyone does. From men who use greasy, sticky, dust-catching pastems (that fool nobody!) . . . to girls who use vegetable and mineral oils which cling and stay only on hair surface and do no real good at all. So, men and women, why not quit kidding youselves? What you need is something similar to the natural oil which assures the health and beauty of your own hair. Only lanolin is exactly that! And you get the most and best of lanolin that your hair can absorb only in Charles Antell Formula 9. This "penetrating lanolin" compound brings your hair new highlights, liveliness, shapeliness, and loveliness almost instantly. And it must work for you as it has for millions of other men and women, or you can get more than your money back. The Antell "minute miracle" is proof positive! Never before have so many people found so great a help for so much improvement in *healthy-hair* beauty in so short a time.

So go to your nearest drug, chain, department store, or supermarket today and get Formula 9. And remember, your progressive barber or beauty shop can give you professional hair care with Charles Antell Formula 9 and Shampoo, too.

### Charles Antell

## FORMULA 9 and SHAMPOO

During this introduction, the regular size Formula 9 plus the gift of the regular 8 oz. shampoo costs only $2. And the large family size, plus gift of 16 oz. shampoo, costs only $3. If for any reason you return the Formula 9 and get your money back, *keep* the gift shampoo . . . and you have, "more than your money back!"

258

## 1952

# This is no shape for a girl.

**That's why Warner's makes the Concentrate girdle and the Little Fibber bra.**

Girls with too much bottom and too little top: Warner's can reshape you.

We reshape you on the bottom with the Concentrate girdle: Its all-around panels do more for you than a little girdle (they're lined up to help you where you need help most), yet Concentrate doesn't squash you like a heavy girdle.

We reshape your top with the Little Fibber bra. The super-soft fiberfill lining doesn't make a big production out of you. It rounds out your bosom just enough to go with your trimmed-down hips.

All of a sudden, you've got a proportioned body, and your clothes fit better. Warner's calls this a Body-Do.™ You can get fitted for one in any good store.

**1967**

**HE**—"That lady has a mustache!"

**SHE**—"How embarrassing!"

**HE**—"Why doesn't she shave?"

**SHE**—"I know a better way to treat that case—listen—I'll tell you a secret—for some years I had a difficult problem of ugly, superfluous hair on face and limbs. I was discouraged—unloved. Tried many different products, but nothing was really satisfactory. Then I developed a simple, painless, inexpensive method—It worked, and brought me happiness."

I have helped thousands seeking a more pleasing appearance free of that ugly, noticeable, unwanted hair. My FREE book, "How to Overcome the Superfluous Hair Problem," explains the method and proves actual success. Mailed in plain envelope. Also trial offer—no obligation. Write Mme. ANNETTE LANZETTE, P. O. Box 4040, Merchandise Mart, Dept. 201, Chicago, Ill.

**1950s**

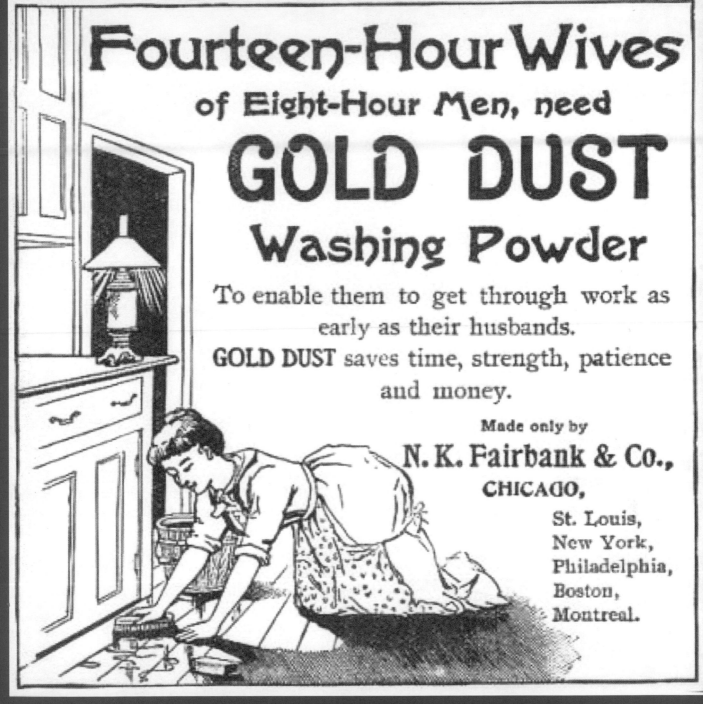

1893

**1930s**

**1974**

**1966**

1970s

1917

The Chef
does everything
but cook
- that's what
wives are for!

I'm giving my wife a

**Kenwood** Chef

**1961**

It's nice to have a girl around the house.

Though she was a tiger lady, our hero didn't have to fire a shot to floor her. After one look at his **Mr. Leggs** slacks, she was ready to have him walk all over her. That noble styling sure soothes the savage heart! If you'd like your own doll to doll carpeting, hunt up a pair of these he-man **Mr. Leggs** slacks. Such as our new automatic wash-wear blend of 65% "Dacron*" and 35% rayon—incomparably wrinkle-resistant. About $12.95 at plush-carpeted stores.

**Dacron** *for Fall*!

*Get yourself a new pair of* **Mr. Leggs**

THOMSON COMPANY, 1290 Avenue of the Americas, New York 19, N.Y.

**1970**

**1940**

# Now You Can Reduce a Bulging Chest-Line

## New Discovery Slenderizes Oversize Bust—Takes Off One To Three Inches

IS YOUR figure marred by a heavy, sagging bust? Does that embarrassing chest-line bulge make you self-conscious and ill at ease?

Now you can *reduce* an oversize bust. You can take *inches* off your chest-line and remould your form to trim, rounded shapeliness. The wonderful FORMULA-X treatment is made expressly to correct this unsightly figure fault. All you have to do is apply Formula-X compound, follow the easy, pleasant instructions and soon the flabby fat begins to disappear. Your bust actually becomes smaller, firmer, more shapely. Sagging tissues are restored to the high, arching position that is so smart and attractive.

## 1930s

# Gray Hair Cost Her Her Job!

She was willing and capable, but gray hair made her look old and slow. "A younger woman would work more snappily," was the verdict.

Gray hair *does* make a person look old, but gray hair is an unnecessary burden. Today, many women—and men—know that a mixture of sage tea and sulphur actually restores gray, faded or streaked hair to its original life and color. You can either prepare the mixture at home yourself, or more conveniently, buy it already prepared and ready to use. All druggists carry it in the form of Wyeth's Sage & Sulphur, and since the cost is only 75c a bottle, there is really no need to prepare it yourself. You simply moisten a comb or soft brush with it and draw it through your hair, one strand at a time. One application banishes the gray and one or two more completely restore your hair to its original color, so evenly, so naturally that no one can possibly tell you have used it.

## 1920s

# If your husband ever finds out

*you're not "store-testing" for fresher coffee...*

*...if he discovers you're still taking chances on getting flat, stale coffee ...woe be unto you! For today there's a sure and certain way to test for freshness before you buy*

# Cigarettes are like women. The best ones are thin and rich.

Silva Thins are thin and rich.
Thin so they taste light.
Lighter than other 100's.
Lighter than most kings.
Rich because—
Well, because rich is better.

## Silva Thins are thin and rich.

**1970**

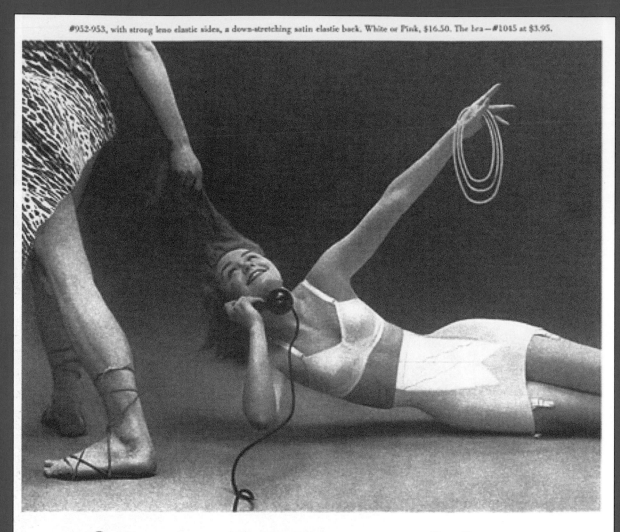

#952-953, with strong leno elastic sides, a down-stretching satin elastic back. White or Pink, $16.50. The bra—#1045 at $3.95.

# Come out of the bone age, darling...

## Warner's exclusive new STA-FLAT replaces pokey bones with circular springlets

WARNER'S takes the cave-man manners out of old-fashioned girdles (poke, shove, groan), removes those long front bones that dug into your midriff. Now control's achieved with light springlets pocketed in the girdle's front panel. They're light and flexible—modern as your way of life, sensible as vitamins.

Far better control, too — STA-FLAT gives not just pinpoint support, like old-fashioned bones, but firms a greater area with lively comfort. Bend, breathe, sit ... STA-FLAT™ moves through the day with you, responds to every movement of your body...all with unbelievable lightness. And at the same time, it gives you extra support where you need it most (midriff, waist, tummy).

You don't need to wear armor to be a charmer. Warner's is happy to give the dino-saur his due—but not on you. Come out beautifully, into the light, free whirl of today! At your nicest stores, here and in Canada.

# WARNER'S®
## Bras · Girdles · Corselettes

**1955**

# *Housewives!*
## PLEASE FINISH TRAVELLING BY
# 4 O'CLOCK
## and leave the buses, trams and trains free for war workers

Issued by the MINISTRY OF TRANSPORT and the MINISTRY OF LABOUR AND NATIONAL SERVICE

## WWII

1954

# 1930s

My wife's joined the Suffrage Movement.
(I've suffered ever since!)

**1910**

# DO YOU STILL BEAT YOUR WIFE?

Maybe you should never have stopped. Read why in the rollicking, provocative, yet educational booklet entitled, "Why You Should Beat Your Wife", written by an eminent practitioner of this manly art. Send 15c in stamps or coin to

## CO-LE SALES COMPANY
538 W. Deming Place, Chicago 14, Illinois

**1930**

**1909**

Right down the Alley...
with a Microsheen Shine!

You'll really bowl 'em over whenever you sport a MICROSHEEN shine. That's because MICROSHEEN is right down the alley when it comes to keeping shoes at their sparkling best. Costlier waxes, rare conditioning oils, wonder-working silicones to impart a long-lasting brilliance under all weather conditions. Buy a can of GRIFFIN MICROSHEEN today. It's a "ten strike" every time!

GRIFFIN MICROSHEEN

**1974**

# 1950s

**1953**

**1953**

# Fashion

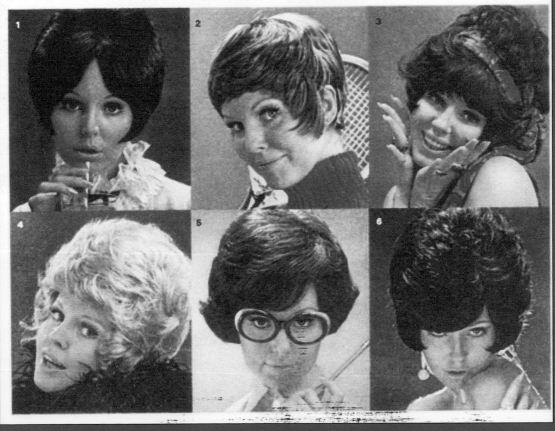

**1970**

# The denim boot is here.

Acme's got 'em. In both Acme® Western boots and Dingo® boots, the boots for everyone. Both are denim on top and tough blue suede cowhide on the foot. They go with all your denims. They go with everything. And since Acme is the world's biggest bootmaker, we can make our new denims with everything a boot should have. At a price that'll leave you with some cash in your jeans.

**acme dingo** more boot for less bucks.

We also make Dan Post® and Hawkeye® boots.

For the store near you, write: Acme Boot Co., Inc., Dept. WH34, Clarksville, Tenn. 37040. A subsidiary of Northwest Industries, Inc.

## 1974

# A NATURAL EXPLOSION FROM AFRO SHEEN.®

Explode your 'fro to new heights with the new Afro Sheen® Blowout Kit. It relieves those excess tangles, while it leaves your hair looking fuller, fluffier and longer. Easier to style too. Here's what you get:
Gloves for application, Mild No-Base Afro Sheen® Blowout Creme Relaxer, Neutralizer Shampoo, new Afro Sheen® No-Rinse Instant Conditioner, Creme Gel (for those sensitive areas) and Afro Sheen® Conditioner and Hair Dress for styling. See? Everything you need. So, if the Fluffy Blowout is your thing, then do it with *our* thing. The New Afro Sheen® Blowout Kit. (BOOM)

Climb aboard the "Soul Train" every week. It's the hippest TV trip in America. (Check listings for time and channel)

**1972**

# THE KING COLLAR!

## $16.95
Two for $32.50

Royal and rich . . . made of a luxury fabric blended of 94% acetate, 6% nylon, with the look and feel of silk jersey. With the amazing KING collar — 12" high in front, 7½" wide, 4¼" high in back, this great shirt will make you stand out in splendor! Flowing puff sleeves, double button front and cuffs, four glowing colors. S674 Black. S675 Blue. S676 Burgundy. S677 White. Sizes: S,M,L,XL. $16.95 ppd., or $2 deposit on C.O.D. — you pay postage. Satisfaction guaranteed. See our collection of dramatically styled apparel and imported footwear.

## Eleganza

1481 Manley St., Brockton, Mass. 02403

**WRITE FOR FREE CATALOG**

# 1970

78

**1971**

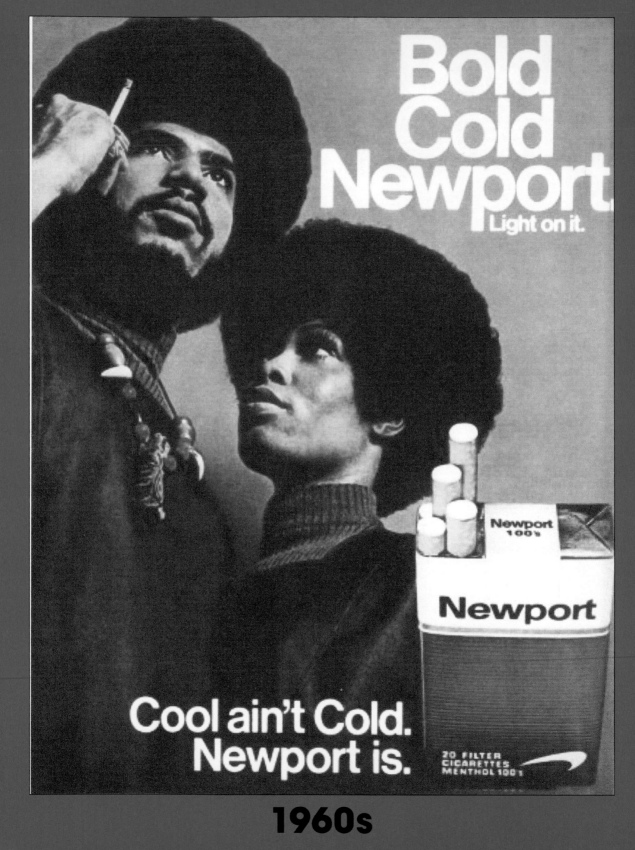

**1960s**

**1965**

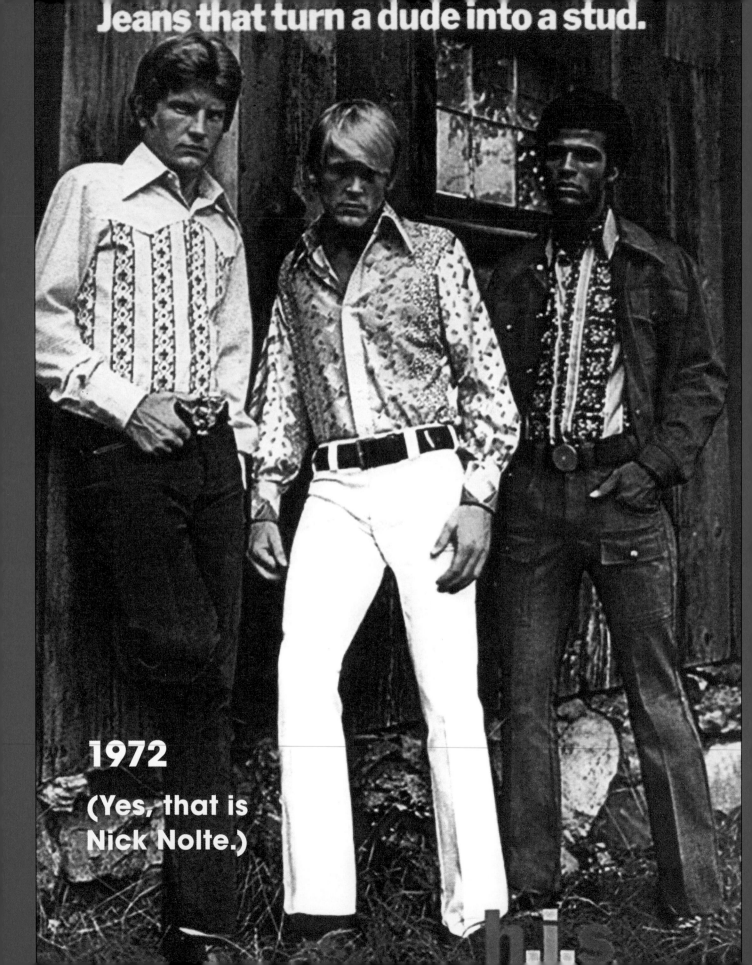

# Medical Claims

**1934**

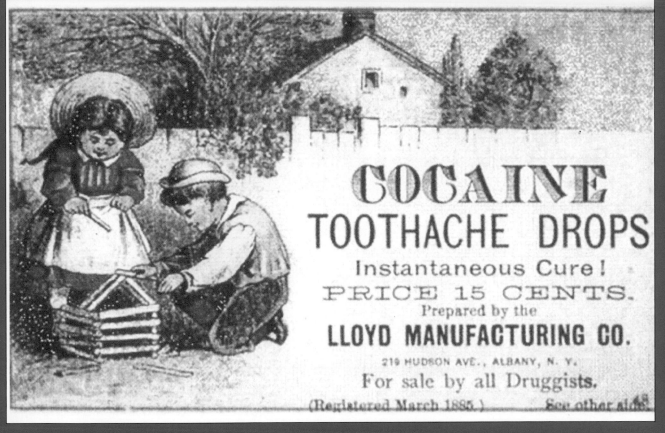

**1900**

**1956**

*Pure pleasure!*

## Seven-Up is so pure...so wholesome!

For a fact, you can even give this sparkling drink to babies—and without any qualms. Lots of mothers do just that!

Just read the ingredients on the 7-Up bottle and you'll see why. We're proud to list them for your inspection, even though regulations don't require this on soft drinks.

Seven-Up has a special fresh, clean taste that appeals to everyone at your house be he nine months, nine years or ninety. It's the All-Family Drink!

*Watch "Soldiers of Fortune" on TV every week. Exciting 7-Up adventure series.*

## Nothing does it like Seven-Up!

**1917**

# Don't Stay Too Fat!

COMFORT, health and fashion demand right physical proportions. You can reduce the flesh on your entire body, or any part, by wearing one of Dr. Jeanne Walter's famous rubber garments for men and women a few hours a day

The safe and quick way to reduce is by perspiration. Endorsed by leading physicians.

Frown Eradicator . . $2.00
Chin Reducer . . . 2.00
Neck and Chin Reducer 3.00
Bust Reducer . . . 5.00
Abdominal Reducer . 6.00

Also Union Suits, Stockings, Jackets, etc., for the purpose of reducing the flesh anywhere desired. Invaluable to those suffering from rheumatism.

Write at once for further particulars

**BUST REDUCER $5.00**
Made from Dr. Walter's famous reducing rubber with coutil back.

**DR. JEANNE K. WALTER**
Inventor and Patentee
45 West 34th Street.     ::     New York

**1925**

# WASH AWAY FAT
## AND YEARS OF AGE

### With La-Mar Reducing Soap

The new discovery. Results quick and amazing—nothing internal to take. Reduce any part of body desired without affecting other parts. No dieting or exercising. Be as slim as you wish. Acts like magic in reducing double chin, abdomen, ungainly ankles, unbecoming wrists, arms and shoulders, large busts, or any superfluous fat on body. Sold direct to you by mail, post paid, on a money-back guarantee. Price 2/- a cake or three cakes for 4/-; one to three cakes usually accomplish the purpose. Send postal or money order to-day. Surprising results. **LA-MAR LABORATORIES, Ltd., 48, Rupert Street (110Li), London. W.1.**

**REDUCE!**

# More than 55% of your daily protein needs

## And a higher level of many vitamins and minerals than the average Australian meal.

Keeping you and your children in good health makes good sense...and good business. And we think our food is as good for you as it is good to eat. We're not suggesting, of course, that a meal at McDonald's gives you all the nutrients you need.

But it is true that a meal of a BIG MAC$_s$, a McDonald's strawberry milk Shake and a (regular) serving of French Fries, provides a substantial proportion of your daily requirements of many nutrients. While this meal combination supplies 40% of the total body requirements of calories, it provides more than 55% of the daily need for protein and greater than 50% of the daily need of many important vitamins and minerals.

The table below indicates specific nutrition information on the illustrated meal.

If you would like further information about McDonald's food, ask at any McDonald's restaurant for our 'Nutritional Look at McDonald's' leaflet. We want you to enjoy our good food... and enjoy it in good health.

**NUTRITION INFORMATION***

The meal combination illustrated here contains the following nutrients in relation to the Recommended Australian Daily Allowances of Protein, Vitamins and Minerals for an average Adult male aged 18 to 35 years. #

| *Protein | 59% | Riboflavin | 44% |
|----------|-----|------------|-----|
| Vitamin A | 18% | Niacin | 33% |
| Vitamin C | 75% | Iron | 54% |
| Thiamin | 25% | Calcium | 77% |

*Nutritional analysis conducted by School of Food Technology, University of New South Wales. Reference: Wills, R.B.H., Greenfield, H. Composition of Australian foods 3. Foods from a major fast food chart. Food Technology in Australia, volume 32, pp 363-366, July, 1980.

#Dietary allowances for use in Australia issued by the Commonwealth Department of Health.

McD3081/80

## 1982

**1913**

1878

This is a peaceful atom working for human health. Its job is to trace how medicines act in the body—where they go, how fast, what they do.

Scientists used this atom in animal laboratory tests on many colds medications —found VapoRub acts faster, hours longer!

*New light on colds...*

# ATOM TRACER TESTS
*prove VICKS VAPORUB*

## acts faster, longer
## than aspirin
## or any cold tablet

When your child has a cold, rub VapoRub over the area of lungs and heart, throat, back and neck. Acts fast!

No other type of treatment relieves all 3 cold areas... nose, throat, chest...all at once; no internal dosing.

VapoRub's medicated vapors relieve throat, head, cough, bronchial congestion. Your child feels good again fast.

While aspirin and cold tablets are still in your stomach...Vicks VapoRub is already treating nose, throat, bronchial area — and keeps bringing relief for hours after tablets have stopped working.

Now — from the laboratories of atomic medicine comes *new proof* of a more effective way you can get relief from miseries of colds.

For scientists have used atom tracer tests to check the action of colds medications—and found that Vicks VapoRub acts faster, longer than aspirin or any cold tablet.

No other type of colds medication treats all 3 cold areas—nose, throat, chest—all at once for hours —without internal dosing.

So it's no wonder that more mothers throughout the world de-

pend on Vicks VapoRub than any other colds medication. Why don't you turn to VapoRub too? Enjoy the fast relief—the peace of mind —VapoRub can bring.

Grown-ups and elderly people throughout the world also prefer VapoRub. It acts faster, works longer than aspirin or cold tablets.

# VICKS VAPORUB

*World's most widely used colds medication*

...as a rub...in steam...in the nose

"Vicks" and "VapoRub" are registered trademarks of the Vick Chemical Co., Greensboro, N. C.

## 1958

# IN A CLASS BY ITSELF —
## The RECTO ROTOR
### THE LATEST AND MOST EFFICIENT INVENTION FOR THE QUICK RELIEF OF
# PILES, CONSTIPATION AND PROSTATE TROUBLE

Lubricating
V e n t
H o l e s

## ACTUAL
## SIZE

*Large Enough to be Efficient Small Enough for Anyone Over 15 Years Old.*

(A) *Unguent Chamber*

(B)

*Registered U.S. Patent Office.*

Recto Rotor
NEW YORK

The RECTO ROTOR is the only device that reaches the Vital Spot effectively. This picture tells its own story Note especially those little vent holes in the nozzle through which the unguent inserted in the chamber below (a) may be forced out by turning the knurled cap (b). No other appliance in the world is so constructed: none other able to reach the Vital Spot to such good purpose.

The RECTO ROTOR obtains its *amazingly quick results* without the use of medicine. electricity. operations. or massage by an attendant. It gets results because of its scientific construction. It is made for the purpose of relieving congestion in the prostate gland, lubricating the colon and massaging the muscles of the rectal region. It is used by the patient himself in the privacy of his own home.

The RECTO ROTOR Lubricating Dilator is the only improvement ever made on the common "dilator" which hitherto was the most successful appliance for the relief of Piles and Constipation.

# 1910

# NATURAL BIRTH CONTROL?

Yes. A more natural form of birth control is possible with Delfen® Contraceptive Foam.

**Doesn't affect your hormones.** Delfen is a vaginal foam made to approximate the natural condition of a normal healthy vagina. Works without affecting your hormones.

**No interruptions.** Delfen may be applied up to one hour before intercourse to avoid interruption, and the temptation to "skip it this time."

**Nothing to interfere with sensation.** Delfen is used all by itself. Without mechanical barriers to interfere or inhibit. This delicately scented, snow white aerosol foam is virtually undetectable in use. It doesn't leak or run.

**Proven effectiveness.** Delfen Foam contains one of the most effective sperm killing ingredients in use today—Nonoxynol 9. And while no method of contraception can guarantee 100% effectiveness for all women, tests on thousands of women plus the experience of hundreds of thousands of users prove Delfen to be highly effective when used as directed.

Delfen Foam forms a protective shield and kills sperm on contact.

Available without a prescription.

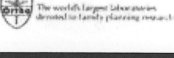

**Delfen.
A natural approach
to birth control.**

ortho The world's largest laboratories devoted to family planning research.

## 1973

# Racist Ads

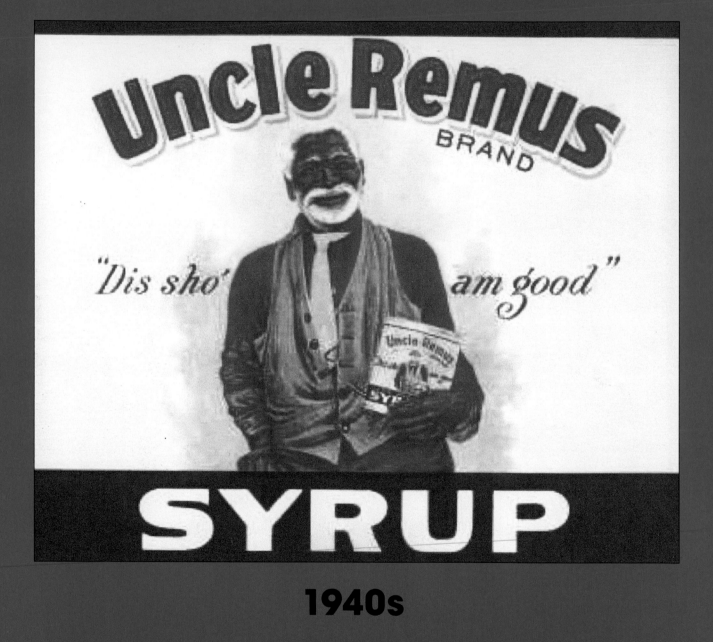

**1940s**

**1921**

**1910**

# AUCTION SALE
### OF
# NEGROS
*This day, at Eleven o'clock, A.M.*
**At the North of the Exchange,**
BY
## J. S. RYAN.

| | | | |
|---|---|---|---|
| 1 | Kate, | Age, | 23 |
| 2 | Sarah, *H Allen* | | 5 |
| 3 | Martha, | " | 2 |
| 1 | Ralph, | Age, | 32 |
| 2 | Unity, *withdrawn* | " | 30 |
| 1 | Juliett, | Age, | 30 |
| 2 | Hetty, *H Allen* | | 60 |
| 1 | Miley, | Age, | 35 |
| 2 | Mary, *no sale* | " | 16 |
| 3 | Julia, | " | 8 |
| 1 | Mary, | " | 35 |
| 2 | Peggy, *H. Allen* | | 17 |
| 3 | Sally, | " | 60 |
| 1 | Rosanna, | Age, | 40 |
| 2 | Paul, | " | 17 |
| 3 | Dinah, *$590 withdrawn* | " | 16 |
| 4 | James, | " | 12 |
| 1 | Rachel, | Age, | 31 |
| 2 | Matilda, *H Allen* | | 14 |
| 3 | Jacob, | | 10 |
| 4 | Frank, | " | 1 |
| 1 | Isabella *H. A* | Age, | 17 |
| 1 | Maria, *H. A* | Age, | 18 |

*March 8, 1855.*

**1855**

**1919**

**1859**

If you know a little Chinese, you might sense these aren't the kindest words you've seen.

Some of our Chinese laundrymen friends have decided to throw in the towel.

It seems this new intruder is quickly becoming a hit with quite a few apartment dwellers, mobile homers, bachelors, and working girls—their usual clientele.

It's the new compact Hoover Washer. That spin-drys, too.

These active people think it's pretty convenient to have around.

They like the fact that it's portable. That they can roll it to any sink and hook it to the faucet. That it's compact enough to store just about anywhere. And, of course, the fact that it beautifully washes, rinses, and spin-drys 6 pounds of clothes in just 6 minutes.

And they certainly don't miss their excursions to damp cellars. Or feeding money

to those coin-hungry washers. Or taking that weekly jaunt out to the nearest Chinese laundry.

So what do the laundrymen have to say about all this?

這敗東西

**1965**

# You don't have to be Jewish

**1961**

# to love Levy's
### real Jewish Rye

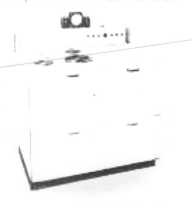

1960

**1938**

# Technology

## "Designing a revolutionary concept in software demanded a computer with extraordinary performance. The Tandy 2000 delivered."

—Bill Gates
Chairman of the Board,
Microsoft

Bill Gates has been at the leading edge of personal computing from the very beginning. His company is a leading producer of microcomputer software.

"Our newest software product, MS-Windows, is an integrated windowing environment. It will let personal computer users combine individual programs into a powerful, integrated system.

"When we set out to design MS-Windows in color, we knew that the Tandy 2000 computer would let us turn an extraordinary product into a work of art. The graphics are sharp and crisp, and gave us a degree of creativity like nothing before.

"Our engineers were quite impressed with the processing speed of the Tandy 2000's 80186 microprocessor, too. And while the finished product will utilize the 2000's Digi-Mouse, the well-laid out keyboard has helped us speed through the design stage.

"We're proud of our work. So when we want to show someone how great MS-Windows really is, we give them a demonstration. On the Tandy 2000."

Isn't it time you enjoyed peak performance from a

personal computer? Go ahead, watch how much faster today's most sophisticated programs run on the high-technology Tandy 2000.

You can choose from the hottest programs around, too, with our exclusive Express Order Software service.

Tandy 2000 systems start at $2999 and can be leased for only $105 per month*. Come in today and see what you've been missing.

Our new 1985 computer catalog is yours for the asking at any Radio Shack Computer Center or participating Radio Shack store or dealer. Check out our complete line of microcomputers — from pocket models to lap-size portables, from powerful desktop computers to multi-user office systems. We have it all. That's why we invite comparison!

**Radio Shack**
COMPUTER CENTERS
A DIVISION OF TANDY CORPORATION

### Engineered for Excellence!
We've introduced the latest in technology for over 60 years. The Tandy 2000 offers twice the speed, graphics resolution and disk storage of other MS-DOS systems.

# 1984

October 16, 1916 THE INDEPENDENT 121

# THE NEW ENLIGHTENMENT

ELECTRICITY comes to free the modern woman from the burdens of housekeeping.

It came into the home first as a source of light, setting a new standard of illumination.

But, electricity is destined to fill a still larger sphere of domestic usefulness; it now does the hardest tasks in the household. It reduces the necessary hours of labor and lightens the nature of the work itself, adding hours to the leisure, recreation, and broader interests that claim the modern woman's attention.

If your home is wired for electricity, are you making the most of it? Do you know the advantages of the electric washing-machine, and the electric iron? Do you know the convenience of the electric toaster and other heating devices for the easy preparation of food?

While other necessaries of life are increasing in cost, electric current is steadily *decreasing*. The cost of using these small devices in the home (never so high as to constitute a serious objection) is now so small as hardly to be reckoned with.

In many parts of the country, rates for electric current are now so attractive as to bring the electric range into very general use for cooking—the greatest boon of all to the housewife.

There is now available for you a complete line of electrical devices bearing the well-known name

**Western Electric**

Every utensil bearing this marking is of highest quality. Write for our literature and the name of our nearest agent in your locality. Ask for booklet, *"The Electrical Way,"* No. 67-BJ.

**WESTERN ELECTRIC COMPANY**

INCORPORATED

| | | | |
|---|---|---|---|
| New York | Chicago | Kansas City | San Francisco |
| Buffalo | Milwaukee | St. Louis | Oakland |
| Newark | Cleveland | Minneapolis | Portland |
| Philadelphia | Detroit | St. Paul | Seattle |
| Boston | Indianapolis | New Orleans | Los Angeles |
| Pittsburgh | Savannah | Houston | Denver |
| Cincinnati | Birmingham | Dallas | Salt Lake City |
| Richmond | Atlanta | Oklahoma City | Omaha |

**EQUIPMENT FOR EVERY ELECTRICAL NEED**

*If your home is not wired for electricity, get an estimate from your contractor. If there is no electric company supplying current in your locality, you can have all these electrical conveniences at small cost through one of our home electric-lighting equipments. Ask us about it.*

# 1906

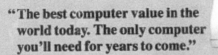
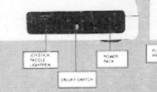
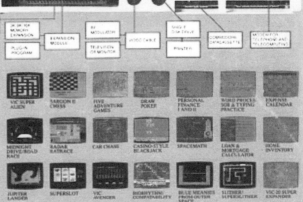

1980

# Can your word processor pass this screen test?

WHAT YOU SEE

IS

WHAT YOU GET

WordStar™ software does*! And does it better than any other word processing system. Not only do you get all the sophisticated features you'd expect from the high-priced WP system, with WordStar you have a true screen image of what your printout will look like **before you print it!**

With WordStar, you'll erase, insert, delete and move entire blocks of copy. Page breaks are

displayed and automatically revised on the screen. You can specify enhancements like underlining and boldfacing, and much more.

And WordStar's so much easier to learn because of its unique and extensive self-help menus. Every typist in your office can be an instant screen star. Call (415) 457-8990 and ask for a copy of our WordStar demon-

stration booklet. Remember, when you're the star, we're the star.

INTERNATIONAL CORPORATION
**The Star Maker**

MicroPro International Corporation
1799 4th Street, San Rafael, CA 94901
(415) 457-8990 TELEX 340388
Sold through authorized dealers and distributors only. OEM inquiries invited

*Runs on most Z80/8080/8085 microcomputers with CP/M (TM of Digital Research), 48K, and terminal with addressable cursor

## 1982

**THE WORLD'S MOST LUXURIOUS
COMMERCIAL AEROPLANE.**

HANDLEY PAGE TYPE W.8,
FITTED WITH 2-450 h.p. NAPIER ENGINES.

**HANDLEY PAGE L**<sup>TD.</sup> **LONDON, ENGLAND.**

## 1930s

**1965**

"What will
the telephone
be like
when
I grow up?"

It's hard to say, young fellow, but you can be sure there are great things ahead.

Today we telephone from moving automobiles, trains, airplanes and ships far out at sea. And radio microwaves beam telephone calls and television programs from tower to tower across the country.

The day is coming when you will be able to reach any telephone in the country simply by dialing a number.

Perhaps some day in the future you may just speak the number into the transmitter and get your party automatically.

BELL TELEPHONE SYSTEM

The Best Possible Service at the Lowest Possible Cost

**1953**

# Hear Muffs. The first headphones you wouldn't kick out of bed.

The worst thing you could take to bed when you're feeling warm and cuddly are cold, lumpy headphones. You'd make out much better with Hear Muffs, the first headphones designed for comfort while lying down— in bed, on a couch, or on the floor.

Hear Muffs don't look like headphones, they look more like a giant fuzzy doughnut with a bite missing. And they don't feel like headphones; your head doesn't get clamped—it gets cradled. You rest on a soft cushion, not a lump of steel and plastic.

Take Hear Muffs to bed soon. The sound is pure and natural, with wide frequency response and minimal distortion. Stereo and 4-channel models from under $30 to under $100. Write us for more information and the name of your local dealer.

## Hear Muffs
513 Rogers St., Downers Grove, Ill. 60515

U.S. & FOREIGN PATE

## 1970s

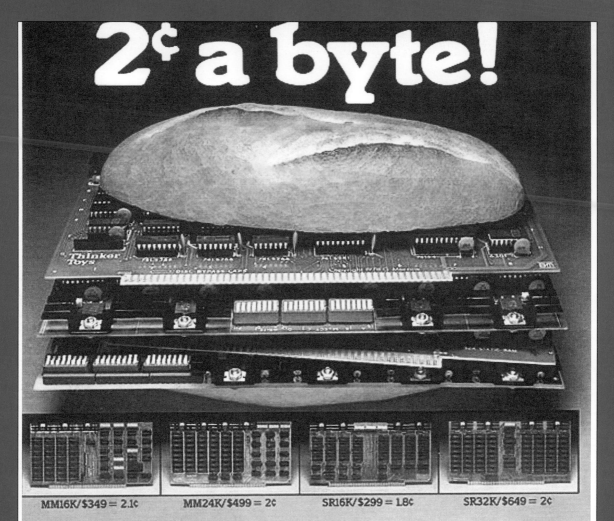

# 2¢ a byte!

| MM16K/$349 = 2.1¢ | MM24K/$499 = 2¢ | SR16K/$299 = 1.8¢ | SR32K/$649 = 2¢ |

**N**ow you can afford to sink your teeth into some big, feature-packed static memories. Because George Morrow's ultra-efficient designs have brought S-100 memory down to 2¢ a byte.

Introducing Morrow's new "MemoryMaster" Bank Select Logic memories, the top of the SuperRam™ line.

The SuperRam™ MemoryMaster 16K Static may be the most sophisticated S-100 memory at any price. The MM16K is switch-programmable to write-protect any of the four 4K blocks ... or to open invisible 1K "windows" to accommodate VDM's or disk controllers. An on-board I/O device and jumper block allow you to use the memory-extending Bank Select Logic features of your software.

Yet, the SuperRam™ MemoryMaster 16K kit is just 2.1¢ a byte at $349. Assembled and tested, $399.

The SuperRam™ MemoryMaster is also available in 24K configuration: 3 individually write-protectable 8K blocks with Bank Select Logic capability. MM24K Kit, $499. Assembled and tested, $549.

Or, get your memory at a rock-bottom 1.8¢ a byte with the SuperRam™ 16K Static. It gives you 4 individual 4K blocks ... plus the ability to switch-enable the Phantom Line for power-up sequencing. Kit, $299. Assembled and tested, $349.

But if you really need a big helping of memory, the SuperRam™ 32K Static serves up two individual 16K blocks for 2¢ a byte: $649 in kit. Assembled and tested, $699.

Whichever Morrow memory suits your taste, it will run perfectly in 2 MHz 8080, 4 MHz Z-80 or 5 MHz 8085 systems. And meets the Proposed IEEE S-100 Standard.

2¢ a byte! That's food for thought. And they're ready to take out at your local computer shop. Or if not, we deliver. Write Thinker Toys,™ 5221 Central Ave., Richmond CA 94804. Or call 415-524-2101 (10-4 Pacific Time any weekday).

*Morrow Designs*
## Thinker Toys™

**1979**

# A color telephone is so <u>beautifully</u> <u>practical</u> in your kitchen

Your kitchen telephone looks so bright and beautiful on your kitchen wall. But it's better than just good-looking— it's one of the most useful appliances you can have. Color telephones make your most-lived-in rooms so much more *livable*. They let you pamper yourself . . . save you time and steps. And they speak so well of your good taste. Drop by or call your telephone business office and ask your Service Representative about them. Learn how little it costs to put color extensions where you need them. Think how very convenient it will be *then* when you make or answer calls.

Enjoy your home with color telephones

Pacific Telephone

Wall phones come in these 7 colors with matching springcords.

## 1958

1982

**1950**

# HOW TELEVISION BENEFITS YOUR CHILDREN

Motorola, leader in television, shows how TV can mean better behavior at home and better marks in school!

**Gets homework done — promptly!** The simple rule "Homework first — television second" has solved the problem in thousands of homes ... has made children more interested in school work. "Television," says the *New York Times*, "can be enjoyed in healthy moderation in the same way as sports or movie-going, but only the mother and father can make certain this will be the case."

**Home, sweet TV home!** Peace! Quiet! No more "rainy day roars" ... with television keeping small fry out of mischief ... and out of mother's hair. And that's just one of many TV blessings. "Taking away television from children who 'act up' is a punishment that really works," writes an authority on child psychology. "The very thought of missing some pet program turns little lions into lambs. And, incidentally, those favorite programs in the late afternoon are the world's finest magnet for getting tardy youngsters home on time."

**Will television strengthen family ties?** Educators, religious and social workers all agree it can be one of the strongest forces in America for bringing the family together to enjoy good, clean entertainment right in the home. Parents can select their children's "TV diet" from a wide variety of wholesome programs.

Motorola's leadership in cabinet design as well as performance is recognized with the 1950 Fashion Academy Gold Medal Award. Typical example of Motorola supremacy is this Table Model 17T1. Clear, steady 16" picture, only 2 simple controls, Built-in Antenna, price only $219.95. View it at your dealer's along with other beautiful Motorola models from $189.95 to $650.00. Then let a Motorola demonstration in your home show you how much TV enjoyment can benefit your own children.

## Motorola
### TELEVISION

# the TV of the future is here today

Some day probably all television will be like the Micro-TV. But today, only with the remarkable SONY can you enjoy "high fidelity picture quality" so obviously superior that all other sets pale in comparison. But picture quality is only one of the unique features. The Micro-TV weighs only 8 lbs., which means it can be carried easily to any room in the house, or to the office as a truly personal set. In addition, since it is fully transistorized (with 3 epitaxial and 5 mesa transistors among its complement of 25), it can be operated on its own rechargeable battery, 12 v auto/boat battery and AC. This means, of course, that it can be used anywhere outdoors, even in a moving auto or on a boat. But since a TV set is only as good as its picture, the inherent superiority of Micro-TV with 70° tube deflection and special SONY-developed phosphors must be seen to be appreciated. Your dealer will be happy to arrange for a convincing demonstration. Micro-TV list $229.95; rechargeable battery, luggage carrying case auto accessory kit extra.

TFM-95—9-transistor FM/AM portable adapts easily as a car radio. Outstanding tone; drift-free AFC; accepts multiplex adapter. Complete with battery. List $79.95. Car bracket $12.95.

TR-817—8-transistor pocketable with tone control, on-off button and tuning meter, offers big set sound quality. Complete with battery, earphone, case, extra antenna. List $39.95.

**SONY®**
RESEARCH MAKES THE DIFFERENCE

For more information on the SONY Micro-TV and transistor radios write to

**1963**

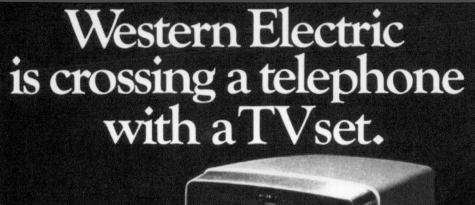

# Western Electric is crossing a telephone with a TV set.

Someday you'll be a star!

What you'll use is called, simply enough, a Picturephone® set. Someday it will let you see who you are talking to, and let them see you

The Picturephone set is just one of the communications of the future Western Electric is working on with Bell Telephone Laboratories.

Western Electric builds regular phones and equipment for your Bell telephone company. But we also build for the future.

**Western Electric**
MANUFACTURING & SUPPLY UNIT OF THE BELL SYSTEM

## 1968

1939

# Low-cost hard disk computers are here

### 11 megabytes of hard disk and 64 kilobytes of fast RAM in a Z80A computer for under $10K. Two floppy drives, too. Naturally, it's from Cromemco.

It's a reality. In Cromemco's new Model Z-2H you get all of the above and even more. With Cromemco you get it all.

In this new Model Z-2H you get not only a large-storage Winchester hard disk drive but also two floppy disk drives. In the hard disk drive you get unprecedented storage capacity at this price—11 megabytes unformatted.

You get speed—both in the 4 MHz Z80A microprocessor and in the fast 64K RAM which has a chip access time of only 150 nanoseconds. You get speed in the computer minimum instruction execution time of 1 microsecond. You get speed in the hard disk transfer rate of 5.6 megabits/sec.

#### EXPANDABILITY

You get expandability, too. The high-speed RAM can be expanded to 512 kilobytes if you wish.

And the computer has a full 12-slot card cage you can use for additional RAM and interface cards.

#### BROADEST SOFTWARE SUPPORT

With the Z-2H you also get the broadest software support in the microcomputer field. Software Cromemco is known for. Software like this:

- Extended BASIC
- FORTRAN IV
- RATFOR (RATional FORtran)
- COBOL
- Z80 Macro Assembler
- Word Processing System
- Data Base Management

with more coming all the time.

#### SMALL, RUGGED, RELIABLE

With all its features the new Z-2H, including its hard disk drive, is still housed in just one small cabinet.

Hard disk drive at lower left can be interchanged just by sliding out and disconnecting plug. Seven free card slots are available. Z-2H includes printer interface card.

Included in that cabinet, too, is Cromemco ruggedness and reliability. Cromemco is time-proved. Our equipment is a survey winner for reliability. Of course, there's Cromemco's all-metal cabinet. Rugged, solid. And, there's the heavy-duty power supply (30A @ 8V, 15A @ +18 V, and 15A @ −18V) for circuitry you'll sooner or later want to plug into those free card slots.

#### CALL NOW

With its high performance and low price you KNOW this new Z-2H is going to be a smash. Look into it right now. Contact your Cromemco computer store and get our sales literature. Find out when you can see it. Many dealers will be showing the Z-2H soon—and you'll want to be there when they do.

> **PRESENT CROMEMCO USERS**
> We've kept you in mind, too. Ask about the new Model HDD Disk Drive which can combine with your present Cromemco computer to give you up to 22 megabytes of disk storage.

## Cromemco
Incorporated

280 BERNARDO AVE., MOUNTAIN VIEW, CA 94040 • (415) 964-7400
Tomorrow's computers now

CIRCLE 135 ON READER SERVICE CARD

# 1975

## 1927

**1981**

# "A Few Years Ago, the Idea of a Computer You Could Put in Your Pocket Was Just Science Fiction."

—Isaac Asimov
Renowned Science and
Science-Fiction Author

---

## Today, Just $169.95 Buys a Radio Shack TRS-80® Pocket Computer—And That's a Fact!

Back when computers filled entire rooms, Isaac Asimov was writing about computers you could hold in your hand. "Radio Shack's TRS-80 Pocket Computer turned my dreams into reality. Now I can take the power of a true computer with me wherever I go," says Asimov.

The TRS-80 Pocket Computer is programmable in BASIC. Isaac, however, would rather write novels than programs. "If you're like me, you'll want to get a low cost interface that lets you use Radio Shack's ready-to-run programs." There are programs for engineering, finances, statistics—even real estate and aviation.

Programs and data stay in memory even when the Pocket Computer is turned off. And it can also function just like a calculator—something a desktop computer can't do.

"With a TRS-80 Pocket Computer, you can hold the future in the palm of your hand." Add our $79.95 Minisette®-9 cassette recorder and a Cassette Interface for $29.95, or a Cassette Interface with built-in printer for $127.95. They're all as close as your nearby Radio Shack store, dealer or Computer Center.

## Radio Shack®
**The biggest name in little computers℠**

Retail prices may vary at individual stores and dealers.

I want a glimpse of the future— send me a TRS-80 computer catalog.

Radio Shack, Dept. 82-A-367
1300 One Tandy Center
Fort Worth, Texas 76102

NAME _____

ADDRESS _____

CITY _____ STATE _____ ZIP _____

1958

# World War II Propaganda

**1940s**

Ach! Those

# AMERICAN HOUSEWIVES

"Are they making it hard for me and my armies!" You're darn right we are, Adolf. We're saving waste fats—from frying and roasting. After we get all the cooking good out of them, we're rushing them to our meat dealers —by the canful. Those fats make glycerine and glycerine makes gunpowder. If we all save as little as one tablespoon a day— we'll soon be blasting you back to Berlin.

**Waste Fats Urgently Needed —Turn Yours in Now**

*Approved by the War Production Board. Paid for by Industry.*

# RAT POISON WANTED

There's only one way to exterminate the slant-eyes — with gunpowder! Your used cooking grease is needed to make gunpowder. Even with rationing, you can save a tablespoon a day. Rush each canful to your meat dealer.

**1940s**

*Approved by W. P. B. Paid for by Industry*

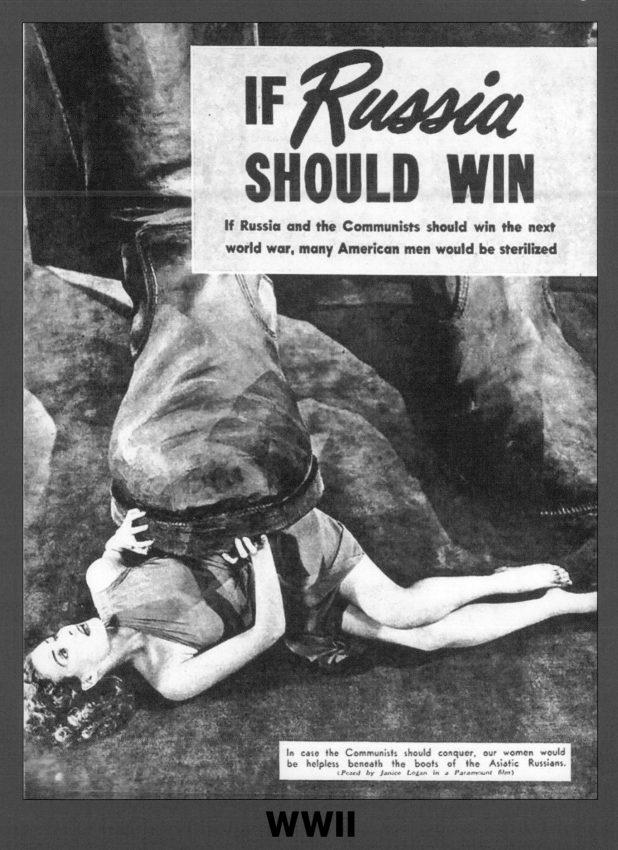

IF *Russia* SHOULD WIN

If Russia and the Communists should win the next world war, many American men would be sterilized

In case the Communists should conquer, our women would be helpless beneath the boots of the Asiatic Russians.
(Posed by Janice Logan in a Paramount film)

# WWII

# Unusual And Shocking Ads

# Don't buy a douche without smelling it first.
# Because that's how you'll smell when you use it.

Send for sample packettes of Jenéen –
the only douche with the scent of fresh lilacs and roses.

To: Mrs. Virginia Drake, R.N.
Dept. C-411, The Norwich Pharmacal Co.
Norwich, N.Y. 13815.

Please send me 4 introductory packettes of
Jenéen. I am enclosing 50¢ to cover the cost of
mailing and handling

Name_____

Street_____

City_____

State_____ Zip Code_____

**np** NORWICH PRODUCTS, division of Morton-Norwich Products, Inc.

162

When you use a douche, you find its scent all
around you...on your body...in the air. That's why we
gave Jenéen* the scent of fresh lilacs and roses.
But that's not why you use it.
You use Jenéen because it cleanses you effectively.
It refreshes you. It helps remove odor. It leaves
you sure of your personal hygiene.
And Jenéen is easy to use. It's a liquid. It mixes
instantly with water. So it can't cake or clump.
And it comes in a convenient bottle as well as
individual pre-measured packettes.
All these things are what douching is about.
The fact that you use Jenéen means you'll
smell as fresh as you'll feel.
And that's what douching's about, too, isn't it?

**1970**

134

# Introducing the Flip'N Style hair dryer. Even if you can't use it it's fun to have.

Of course, it dries your hair. If you happen to think that hair is fashionable. But it's also a nice replacement for your teddy bear. It comes in three terrific colors to go with any bedspread. And it doesn't just sit around like your old teddy.

Because the Flip'N Style™ flips for you. Open. And closed. So when you're through drying (your fingernails, if your hair hasn't grown in), slip it into its attractive case. Then slip it into your attractive purse. So if you run into a cloudburst or fall into a swimming pool, you're prepared.

The Flip'N Style™ has what you need to style your hair. 350 watts of hot-air power. And a switch to turn on cool air when your hair is dry, but not completely styled.

So give your hair a chance. Let it have as much fun as the rest of you. With a Panasonic Flip'N Style.™

## Panasonic.
just slightly ahead of our time.

200 Park Ave., N.Y. 10017. For your nearest Panasonic dealer, call toll free 800 243-6000. In Conn., 1-800 882-6500.

**1972**

1904

**1942**

1955

# You see so many good things in Du Pont Cellophane

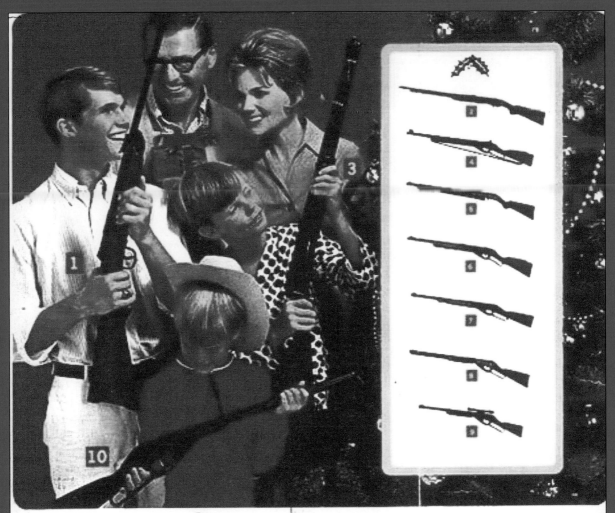

# Seven to seventeen...
# DAISY will make it a Christmas to remember

Whether you're just starting out . . . or graduating to a highpower pellet plinker . . . Daisy's got the right gun for you. You'll have years of fun shooting outdoors or in your own basement or rec room with Mom and Dad. (In fact, we bet Dad can still remember the fun he had with his DAISY.) Show them these beauties and see if they don't agree—the DAISYS are better than ever!

**1 DAISY Pellet Rifles,** Long 'n lean with genuine hardwood stocks and precision steel barrels.

**Model 210** (shown) shoots .22 cal. pellets accurately up to 150 feet. About $15.95.

**Model 220** shoots .22 cal. pellets accurately up to 50 feet. About $13.95.

**Model 320,** top target accuracy up to 90 feet with .177 cal. pellets. About $19.95.

**Model 100** shoots .177 pellets, BBs, darts up to 450 fps. About $14.95.

**2 Model 26 Masterpiece,** "Spittin' Image" of the famous Remington® slide action .22 repeater. 12-shot. About $17.95.

**3 Model 1894,** 40-shot lever action "Spittin' Image" of the rifle that won the West. About $15.95.

**4 Model 99 Target Special,** approved National Rifle Association trainer. Wood stock and forearm. 50-shot. About $14.95.

**5 Model 25 Pump Gun,** a favorite for more than 50 years. 50-shot. About $13.95.

**6 Model 96 Monte Carlo**-styled real wood stock. 700-shot repeater. About $13.50.

**7 Model 95 Woodstock,** handsome sporter styling. 700-shot. About $10.95.

**8 Model 111 Western Carbine** has simulated engraving. 700-shot. About $8.95.

**9 Model 104 Scope Gun** has steel jeep scope. 40-shot. About $7.95.

**10 Model 102** wood stock, short length. 500-shot. About $6.95.

See 'em all at your DAISY Dealer—or write for free 36 page catalog to: DAISY Manufacturing Company, Box 1290, Rogers, Arkansas 72756.

DAISY
MANUFACTURING COMPANY

*Used with permission of Remington Arms Company, Inc.

## 1966

"SCREWDRIVER" DOUBLE-PARKING—*Sure* he could find a place at the curb—but not right where he wants it! His abandoned buggy causes *plenty* of Stop-and-Go, and other drivers pay and *pay* and PAY. Just remember, your engine uses *3 times* as much gasoline in low and second as in high—when a "Screwdriver" brings you to a needless stop, it shows on *your* gas gauge!

# Stop TRAFFIC BONERS—Join the SHARE-THE-ROAD CLUB

"A substantial part of all 'stop-and-go'—25% is a fair estimate—is the direct result of inconsiderate driving manners. Improper parking, for example, greatly impedes the flow of traffic."

*Hawley Briggs*

Traffic Engineer, American Transit Association

From Shell's traffic and engineering studies came the gasoline refined to cut the *cost* of Stop-and-Go driving—Super-Shell!

Now comes a nation-wide crusade to cut the *amount*—by 25%!

Crack down on "Screwdrivers"! To do your part, join Shell's Share-the-Road Club for common sense behind the wheel!

See your Shell dealer today! He'll put the Share-the-Road emblem on your car FREE—give you a booklet showing how traffic boners *increase* your time-wasting, fuel-wasting Stop-and-Go *needlessly*.

"SHARE THE ROAD" AND SUPER-SHELL BOTH SAVE ON STOP-AND-GO

SHOW YOUR COLORS—"SHARE THE ROAD"—CUT STOP-AND-GO DRIVING 25%

ZV 57

**Your Shell Dealer is Headquarters for Saving on STOP-and-GO**

He's a good neighbor—friendly and willing—ready to give your car complete care!

# 1939

1964

**1962**

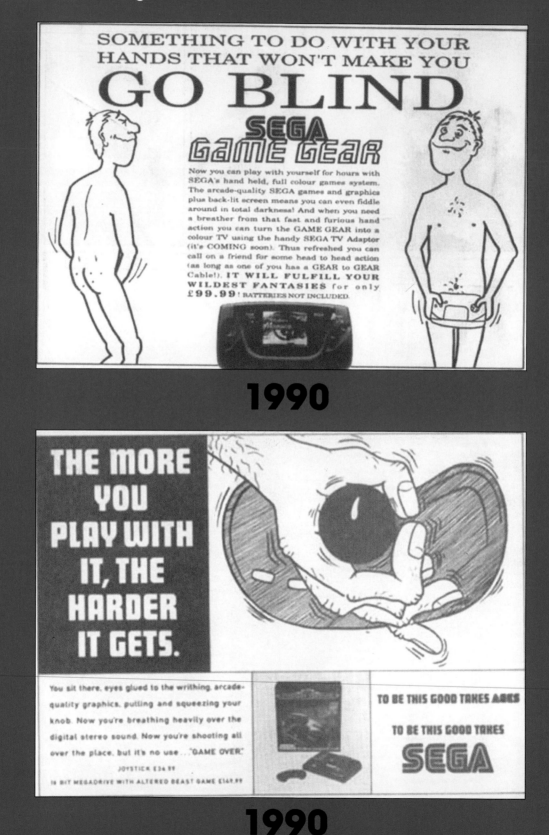

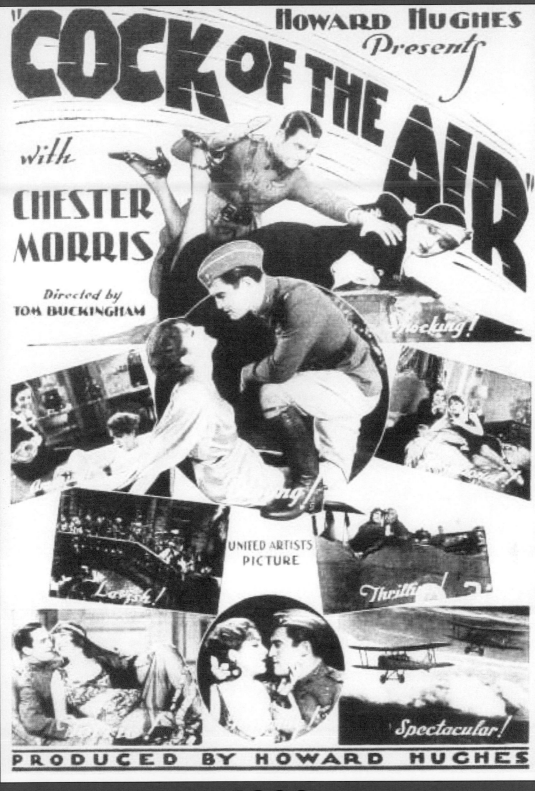

1932

**1950s**

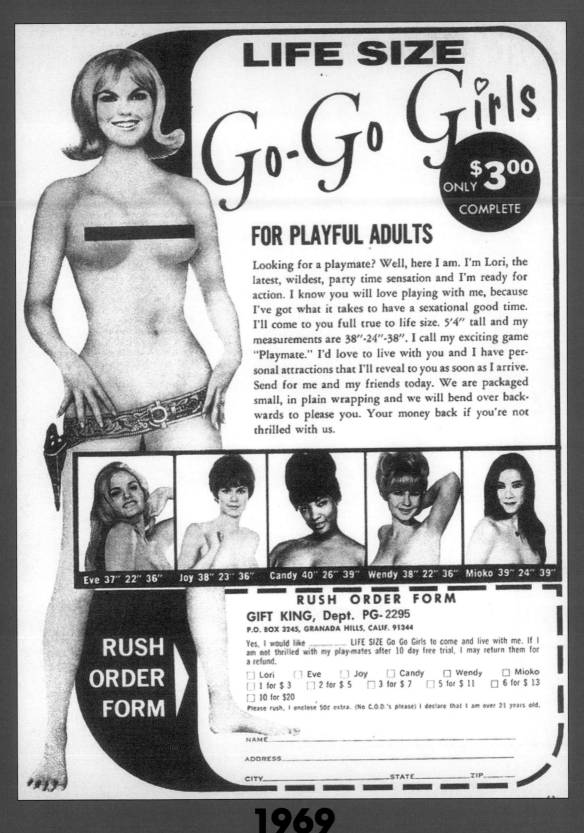

**1969**

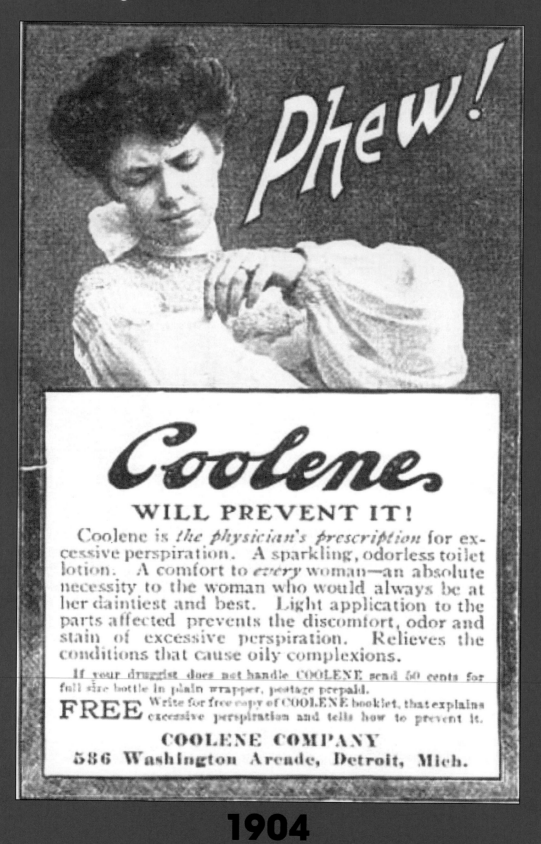

1904

**1936**

**1926**

# "Let's Get Down to Business"

● "STRETCHY-SEAT" is a Munsingwear exclusive. It is a special horizontal panel knitted to give up and down. No other underwear has "STRETCHY-SEAT." Men find it so comfortable they keep coming back for more. That's good business.

"Stretchy-Seat" is an exclusive feature of Munsingwear skit-Trunks, Shorts, Longees and Shin-tights.

# MUNSINGWEAR'S
## "STRETCHY-SEAT"
### UNDERWEAR FOR MEN

1960s

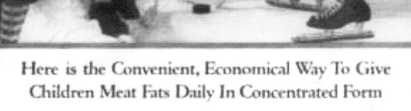

**1920s**

1946

**1959**

**1977**

# Nostalgia

**1960s**

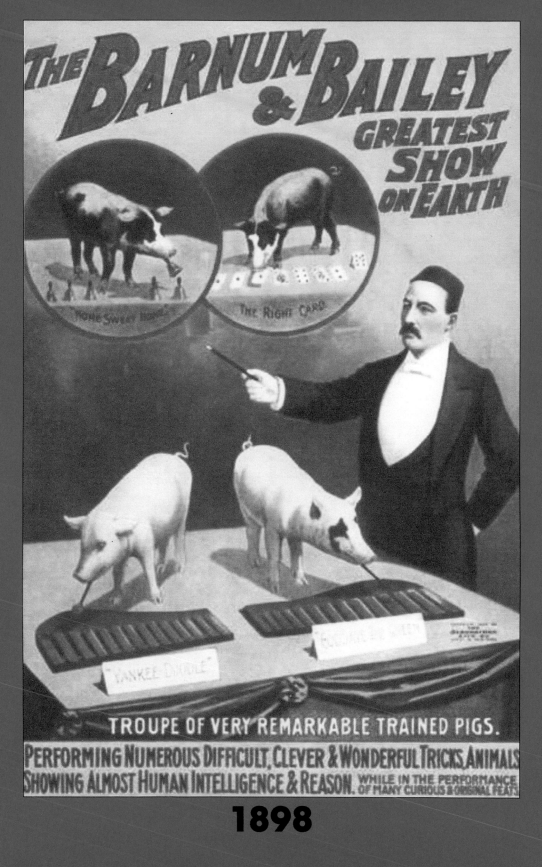

1898

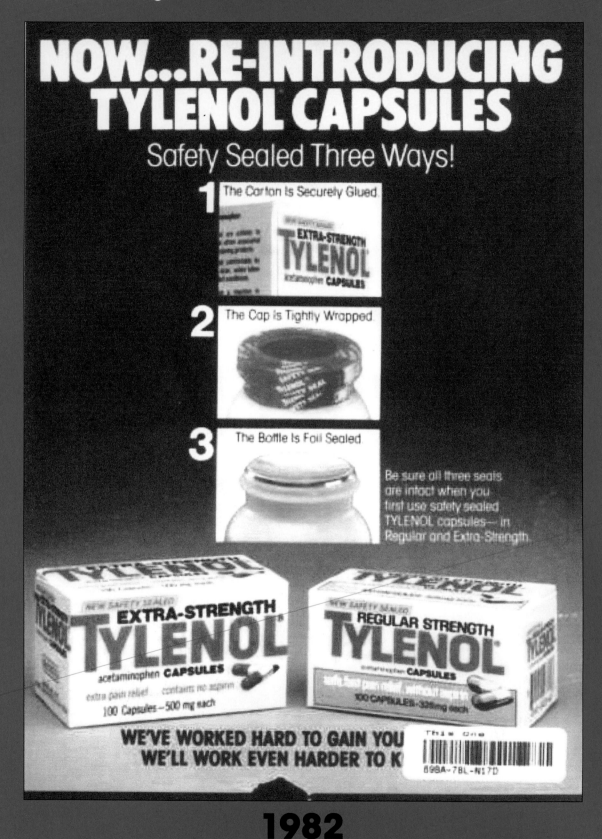

**1982**

1977

**1960s**

# How to catch the early, early show with an easy, easy dinner

**Swanson TV Brand Dinners, the oven-quick meals that taste home-cooked**

Now Mom's in on the TV fun at the start, and thanks to Swanson she's ready to serve an extra-special chicken dinner: Genuine Swanson TV Brand, the frozen dinner that gives you more for your money than any other kind.

Who else but Swanson always gives you three such choice, luscious pieces of chicken? (A rich portion of breast, meaty wing, and a plump thigh or drumstick.) Who else makes fluffy mashed potatoes like this, with milk and creamery butter? Who else gives you buttered, garden-good mixed vegetables like these, with the crispness and tenderness a good cook prizes? (And how that skillful, careful Swanson cookery will remind you of your own!)

Try Swanson TV Brand Dinners. Compare the difference in those generous servings, cooked and seasoned as only Swanson knows how. Four delicious varieties: chicken, turkey, beef, filet of haddock. Ready in 25 minutes or less—no work, no dishes. Remember, insist on genuine Swanson TV Dinners, and always keep a supply handy in your freezer.

QUICK FROZEN BY SWANSON

CHICKEN

TV DINNER

## SWANSON
### T.V. Dinners
MADE ONLY BY Campbell SOUP COMPANY

"TV" and "TV DINNER" ARE REGISTERED TRADEMARKS

## 1954

# Acknowledgments

We would collectively first like to thank Joseph Craig and the fine folks at Skyhorse Publishing for their stalwart work, counsel, and support for this book.

Also, I, Mike, would like to thank Steve, my coauthor and great friend who saw the merit of this idea early on and gave me much-needed feedback when I was too firmly set in my ways regarding its scope and vision. I would like to thank my friends and family for encouraging and supporting me—especially my wife Amy, and daughters Samantha and Sydney, for allowing me to hog the laptop to work long into the night, finding the next startling advertisement. To Marilyn Allen, literary agent extraordinaire— thanks for your support and counsel for more than twenty years. Finally, thanks to my Fordham communications professors, who first taught me about advertising and promotion, and who pushed me to push myself and be a better writer.

And I, Stephen, would like to thank his redoubtable coauthor Mike Lewis for having the idea to do this book and then contributing his keen sense of irony and the ridiculous to the ad selection process. I would also like to thank my main squeeze Valerie, my literary agent John White, my sister Janet, my dear friend and coauthor Rachel, and all who have attended my lectures on *Outdated Advertising*: I can still hear your gasps and laughter upon seeing some of these amazing (in all sense) ads.

# About the Authors

**MICHAEL LEWIS** is a twenty-year veteran of the book publishing business, having acquired, developed, and edited hundreds of successful nonfiction titles for several publishers, both large and small. He is the author or coauthor of ten books, including *A Guy Walks Into a Bar*, *The 100 Best Beatles Songs* (with Stephen Spignesi), and *The Films of Harrison Ford* (with Lee Pfeiffer). He teaches classes at adult schools, including his most successful one on How to Get a Book Published. He lives in northern New Jersey.

**STEPHEN SPIGNESI** is the author of more than seventy books and a retired practitioner in residence from the University of New Haven. Spignesi is considered an authority on the work of Stephen King, the history of the *Titanic*, the music and history of the Beatles, Robin Williams, and the American presidents and Founding Fathers. Spignesi's book *JFK Jr.* was a *New York Times* bestseller. Spignesi's Skyhorse books include *499 Facts About Hip-Hamilton and the Rest of America's Founding Fathers*, *In the Crosshairs*, and *Big Book of UFO Facts, Figures and Truth*. Steve appears in the 2015 ITV documentary *Autopsy: Robin Williams*. His novel *Dialogues* was hailed as a "reinvention of the psychological thriller." Steve lectures extensively on a wide range of subjects, from history to pop culture. He lives in New Haven, Connecticut.

Steve and Mike have written a Beatles-themed screenplay entitled *Pilgrim's Landing*, and are collaborating on a comedy-musical *The Ensorcelled Undertaker*.